ABSURDITIES

MATERNAL INSTINCT

ABSURDITIES

W. HEATH ROBINSON

DUCKWORTH

Fourth impression 1990

This edition first published in 1975 by
Gerald Duckworth & Co. Ltd.
The Old Piano Factory
43 Gloucester Crescent, London NW1

Second impression 1977
Third impression 1979

© 1975 Oliver Heath Robinson

ISBN 0 7156 1583 1

Absurdities was compiled by Heath Robinson himself at the height of his fame and was the only large-scale general collection of his humorous work published during his lifetime. When it first appeared in 1934, there was a limited edition of 250 copies signed by the artist, in addition to two ordinary, popular editions.

 In this reissue nine of the *Absurdities* drawings which have already been reprinted in *Inventions* (1973) are replaced with new material which has not so far appeared in any of his books. The nine old drawings are 'How Noah Averted a Catastrophe', 'Sale-time Improvements', 'Testing Scent Discrimination in Young Foxhounds', 'Multi-Tennis', 'Clam Spearing in the Frozen North', 'Testing Artificial Teeth in a Modern Tooth Works', 'A Surprise Packet for the Cat Burglar', 'Modesty' and 'Kinematographing the Crocodile'. These appear (some with slightly different titles) on pp. 64, 112, 45, 18, 38, 59, 136, 127 and 42 of *Inventions*. The nine new drawings for *Absurdities* are those appearing here on pp. 11, 15, 18, 49, 53, 55, 69, 80 and 91.

Printed in Great Britain
by Unwin Brothers Limited
The Gresham Press, Old Woking, Surrey, England
A member of the Martins Printing Group

WHITHER?

CONTENTS

CONTENTS

AN INTERESTING AND ELEGANT APPARATUS DESIGNED TO OVERCOME ONCE FOR
ALL THE DIFFICULTIES OF CONVEYING GREEN PEAS TO THE MOUTH

7

THE HOLE IN THE SPORRAN
A tale of accumulating interest

PLUCKY ATTEMPT TO RESCUE A FAMILY OVERTAKEN BY THE TIDE

9

HOW TO OBTAIN A GOOD NIGHT'S SLEEP IN SPITE OF INTERRUPTIONS

MODESTY

THE GHOST

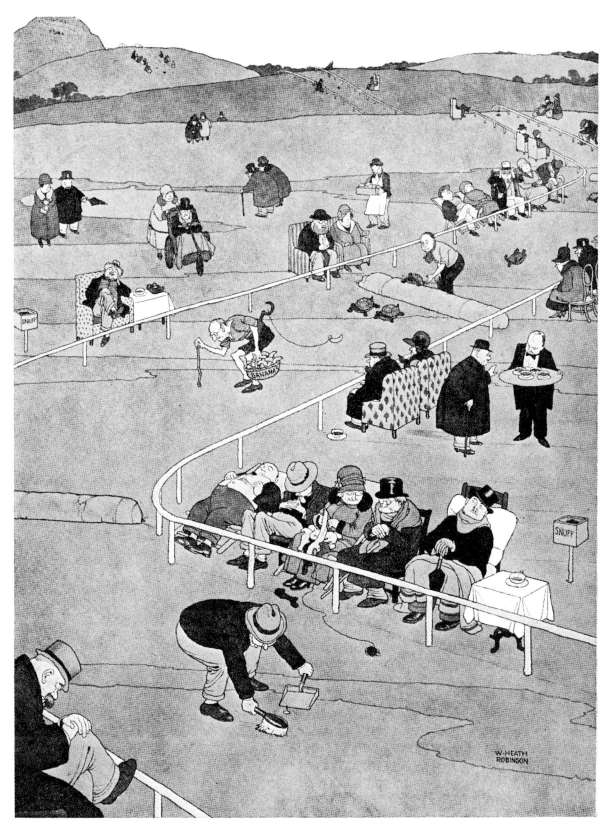

TORTOISE COURSING
A pastime for the peacefully disposed

13

SPOILT CHRISTMASES

HOW TO TAKE ADVANTAGE OF THE SAVOY ORPHEAN DANCE MUSIC

15

THE GUILDHALL OF LONDON
On the eve of the Lord Mayor's Banquet

LAYING THE FOUNDATION STONE OF THE PROJECTED NEW STRUCTURE TO
REPLACE WATERLOO BRIDGE

THE PUNCTURE

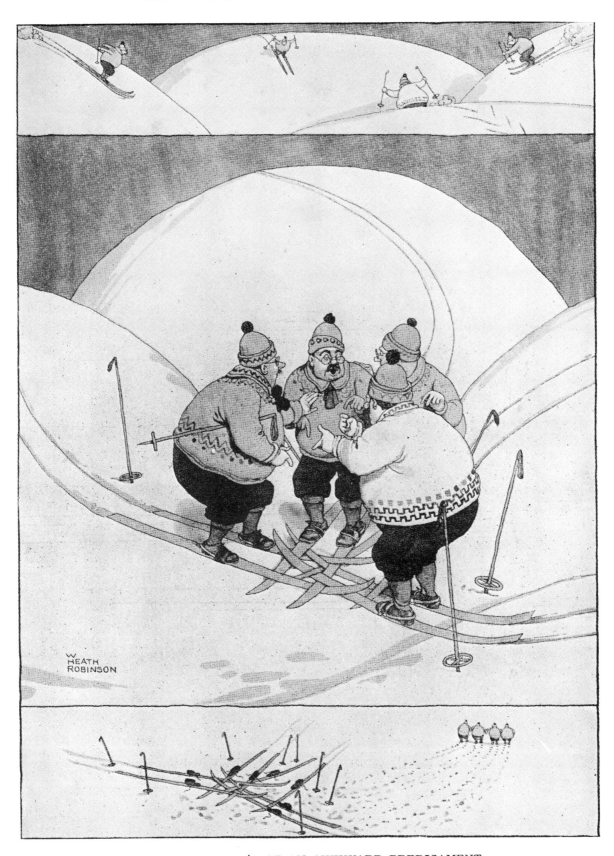

THE ONLY WAY OUT OF AN AWKWARD PREDICAMENT

19

THE NEW MEASURING CHAIR NOW IN USE BY MOST
WEST-END TAILORS

A BUSY MORNING IN THE SUMPTUOUS STUDIO OF A FASHIONABLE HAIR ARTIST

THE EYE OF THE LAW

THE NEW SAFETY-FORK ADJUSTMENT FOR MOTOR-CARS FOR THE PROTECTION OF
CHICKENS ON THE ROAD

HOW THEY PUT THE TARTANS ON THE KILTS IN AN
OLD KILT-WORKS IN THE HIGHLANDS

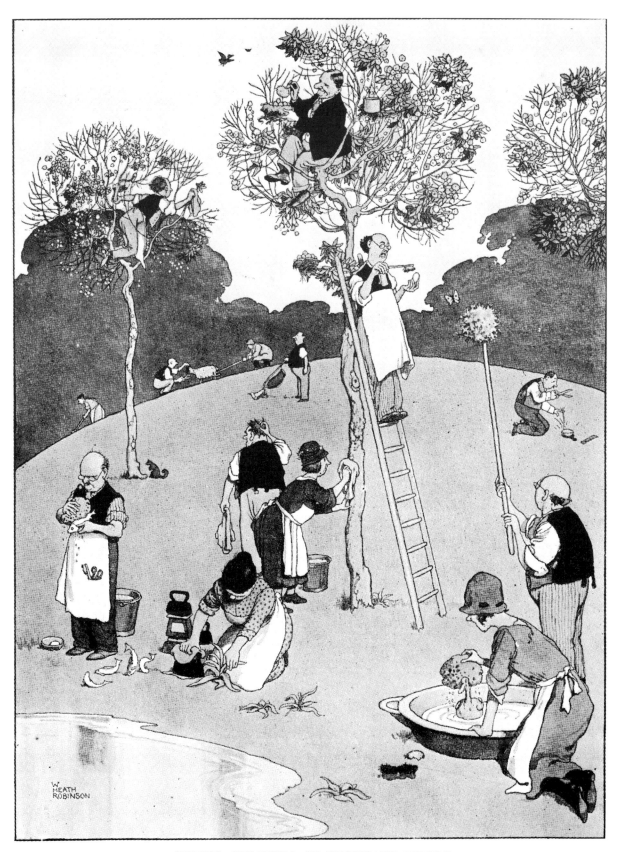

SPRING CLEANING IN HIGHGATE WOODS

CHUTNEY SAUCE NOTES

INCURABLE !

COQUETTE

DOUBLE CROSS TENNIS

For economising space in local tournaments and generally gingering up the game

JUST A PICNIC AT WHIPSNADE

THE NEW BANTING BED FOR REDUCING THE FIGURE

HOISTING THE CHAPERONE

FLAT LIFE

Some ingenious devices for use on chilly mornings

TESTING THE WATERPROOF QUALITIES OF UMBRELLAS
IN AN UP-TO-DATE BROLLEY WORKS

FLAT LIFE

How at last it is possible to keep chickens in the top flat

THE WATER COUPE
An elegant little car for the convenience of anglers

FLAT LIFE
The spare bedroom

SAFETY FIRST!

New road regulations shortly to be introduced to ensure the
safety and comfort of pedestrians

FLAT LIFE

How the tenant of the top flat can enjoy all the amenities of a back garden

FIXING UP THE NEW AERIAL

FLAT LIFE
Sane economy of space at a wedding reception

MAGNETIC AIDS TO SKATERS
To be installed in the London parks during the skating season

FLAT LIFE
How sport is possible on a Saturday afternoon

CHRISTMAS EVE AND THE TOY RAILWAY

44

SUCCESSFUL OUTCOME OF INTELLIGENT PRECAUTION OBSERVED BY OLD LADY
IN THE SOUND OF MULL

REMARKABLE PRESENCE OF MIND OF A CINEMATOGRAPHER
WHO TOOK AN INTERESTING CLOSE-UP OF HIMSELF DURING
AN ACCIDENTAL FALL FROM THE TOP OF BEACHY HEAD

INTERESTING TREATMENT OF CATTLE ON AN ARGENTINE STOCK FARM TO MAKE
THE MEAT TENDER AND SOFT BEFORE KILLING

UNDER THE MISTLETOE
Any old excuse !

TOEING FOR CRABS AT HERNE BAY

49

LOW CUNNING OF A COMMON PICTURE-POSTCARD THIEF

A WARM-HEARTED OLD SOUL DISGUISED AS A MERMAN SEEKING TO LURE A
MERMAID FROM HER NATIVE ELEMENT

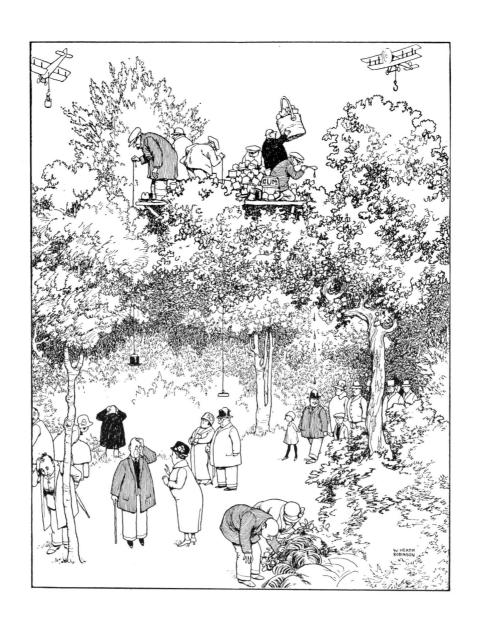

A NOTORIOUS GANG OF HAT THIEVES AT WORK IN EPPING
FOREST ON SUNDAY AFTERNOONS

FOR THE CONVENIENCE OF BATHERS IN ROUGH WEATHER

AN AWKWARD PREDICAMENT

NEW TOP FLAT RESCUE APPARATUS

THE MULTI-MOVEMENT TABBY SILENCER

This apparatus can be operated from the bedroom window and is
guaranteed to reach any part of the back yard

HALF-HOURS AT A MATTRESS-MAKING FACTORY

EARLY MORNING AT SCOTLAND YARD

Detectives in various disguises and the Flying Squad starting out
on their morning rounds

THE STILL SMALL VOICE

Mrs. Blendlethorpe : "For goodness' sake, John, wake up at once ; there's someone calling for help in the room beneath."

THE MAN WHO COULDN'T AFFORD TO
GO TO THE ACADEMY

THE WART CHAIR
A simple device for removing a wart from the top of the head

LUNCHEON HOUR ON THE THAMES EMBANKMENT

HISTORY REPEATS ITSELF
An unrecorded panic at Whipsnade, owing to a spell of wet weather

SELLING IRISH SWEEPSTAKE TICKETS UNDER THE
EYES OF THE LAW

SWIMMING THE CHANNEL
Some simple devices to ensure success

SPRING AND SPRING ONIONS
An idyll of the sea

RESUSCITATING STALE RAILWAY SCONES FOR REDISTRIBUTION
AT THE STATION BUFFETS

THE KIND OF THING WE MUST EXPECT WHEN IT
BEGINS TO FREEZE

SQUARE PEGS INTO ROUND HOLES

THE LANGUAGE OF EGGS

Some new designs for Easter eggs to facilitate the exchange of graceful
sentiments and amorous messages

TEMPERING THE WATER TO THE SHORN LAMB
The new waterside geyser for the holidays

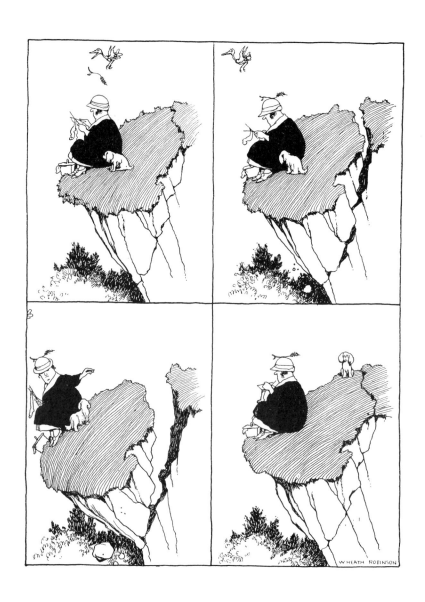

THE LAST STRAW THAT DIDN'T BREAK THE
CAMEL'S BACK

FISH TENNIS
A thrilling new water game

73

THE STOLEN QUEUE

A NEW SNOW-PLOUGH FOR CLEARING A FOOTPATH AFTER A HEAVY FALL

NEW AND INGENIOUS METHODS OF ADVERTISING

A NEW METHOD OF TEACHING WOULD-BE ANGLERS TO ANGLE

ARRIVAL OF THE JUDGE, JURIES, COUNSEL AND
LITIGANTS AT THE LAW COURTS

TRAPPING THE CLOTHES MOTH IN THE WILDS OF IDAHO

MECHANICAL AIDS FOR CHRISTMAS

WHAT SHALL I PUT ON?

Bedside contrivance for the changeable season, to indicate the state of the weather and what you should wear when you get up in the morning

A NEW MACHINE ERECTED ON MARGATE SANDS FOR
DRYING THE HAIR AFTER BATHING

SOME OCCASIONS WHEN A GENTLEMAN IS NOT EXPECTED TO GIVE UP HIS
SEAT TO A LADY

SOMETHING ON EACH WAY
A Fish Tragedy

CULTIVATING BUOYANCY, TOUGHNESS AND RESISTING POWER IN HIDES FOR
FOOTBALLS IN THE STOCKYARDS OF A FOOTBALL FACTORY

THE HOME-MADE CHRISTMAS PRESENT

THE PASSING CLOUD

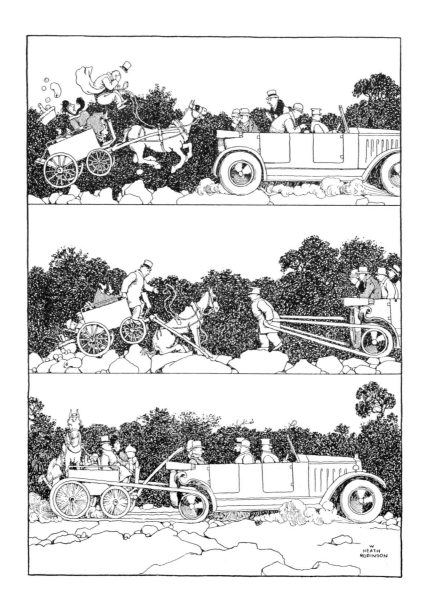

ELASTICITY

Disinterested conduct of kind-hearted motorists to sufferers from the
bad state of the road

OFF TO THE SKI PICNIC

THE SAFETY DECK CHAIR FOR GIVING DUE WARNING
OF THE APPROACH OF THE TIDE

ADVERSE CRITICISM OF STATUARY

STEP THIS WAY

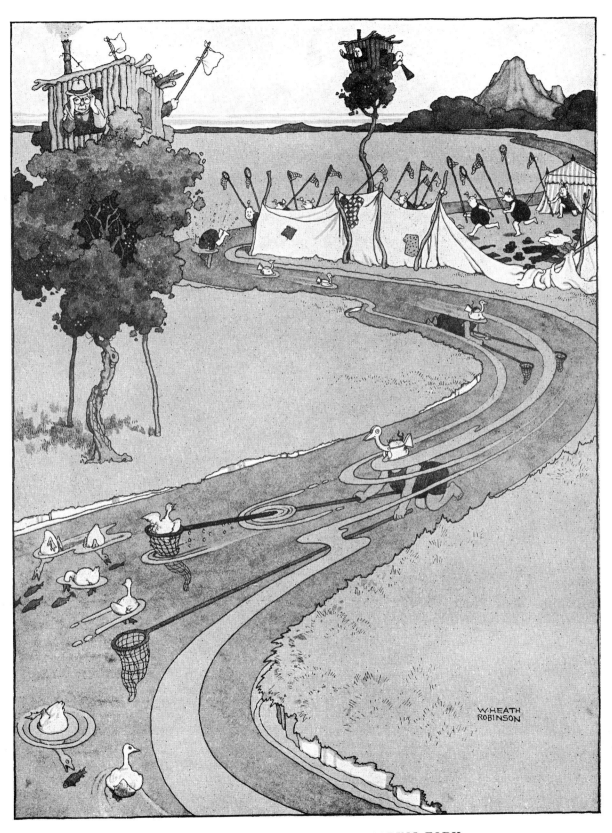

WIDGEON BLUFFING ON THE ROARING FORK

OVERCOMING THE DIFFICULTIES OF SERENADING
IN NEW YORK CITY

STOLEN KISSES

WIRELESS ENTHUSIAST
(*to sympathetic neighbour*)

"Yes, it's quite all right in theory, but somehow or
other in practice the darned thing won't work"